Bert Bielefeld – Roland Schneider

Budgeting

Bert Bielefeld – Roland Schneider

Budgeting

BIRKHÄUSER

BASEL

Contents

Foreword

The key part of an architect's job, alongside design and planning work, lies in managing matters relating to the project and the client. This includes organizational, technical and financial aspects: from planning the sequence of events, tendering, deadline planning and costing via site management to handing over to the client. Here efficient and successful building project management relies essentially on the confident handling of building costs and deadline planning.

It is the planner's duty to deploy the client's money for the building work as the client intended. As a ruler the planner has a pre-arranged budget that he has to distribute between all the costs generated in the course of the work undertaken. Keeping to the prescribed budget is usually crucial to the success of the project as a whole.

For this reason, the quality of planners is assessed to a very considerable extent by the way they control costs and meet deadlines; to an even greater extent, budgeting is one of the most important bases for project realization, and it must play an integral part in the planning and building process. Determining costs is essential when compiling a project budget and for monitoring costs during the subsequent process, so that any costs exceeded during planning and building can be identified and controlled.

As students and professionals at the start of their career have little practical experience, they are particularly uncertain about handling costs for their early building projects. But their responsibility to the client requires that these matters should be tackled confidently.

Basics Budgeting explains budgeting processes during the planning and building phases step by step and in practical terms, and shows in a comprehensive and clearly structured way how cost influences and risks are estimated and evaluated. This is supported by practical tips, examples and simple, comprehensible graphics that help when compiling a budget. Inexperienced planners acquire an indispensable tool for starting work in the budget management field on a sound and practical basis.

Bert Bielefeld, Editor

Introduction

Estimated and actual costs are a key topic for client and architect in many building projects. This is not least because the client has to invest a considerable sum in a building project, a sum that in many cases is far larger than other expenditure. It is therefore essential for the client that contractors work within budgets. This applies particularly when money is being invested in properties to provide a return on investment, where subsequent income (such as rents or sales) is set against the necessary expenditure (building costs, financing costs, depreciation, maintenance costs). The yield or profit (income minus expenditure) from property investments is a key criterion in deciding in favour of the project, and in its success. Even slight building price rises during the construction phase can drag the project into loss – with consequences that can last for many decades.

An additional factor is that construction projects – unlike industrial production – are usually highly individual in character, or can even be like prototypes. This means that processes and structures can be carried over unmodified from one project to another only to a limited extent, so imponderables and surprises may occur that affect timing or finance in a way that was wholly or partly unforeseen at the beginning of the project. Additionally, a lot of time can elapse between deciding in favour of a project and completing the building, so that estimates made at the beginning of the project about shifts in market prices, for example, may sometimes not hold good over a period of time.

Even if this time span can entail considerable financial fluctuation, it is very short if measured against the life cycle of a building, but will still make a substantial impact. Financial decisions, e.g. about options for construction or domestic services, have an effect throughout the entire use or life cycle of the building, and lead to differing running costs. If the costs generated (heating, water and power supplies, repairs, maintenance etc.) while the building is being used are added up, they will be substantially greater than the initial investment. But investment in a building project has to be raised within a very short period of a very few months or years, while running costs extend continuously over decades. Higher initial investment in technical equipment, such as more efficient heating systems, for example, can achieve significant savings within the lifetime of the building. > Fig. 2

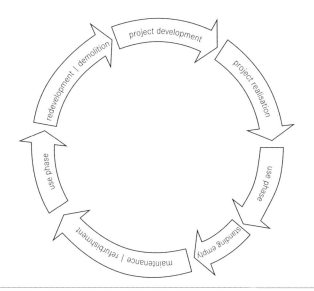

Fig. 1: Life cycle costs

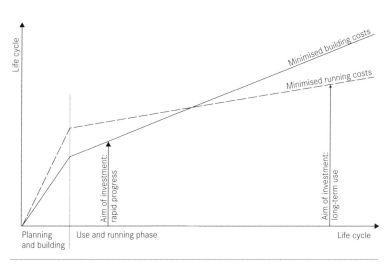

Fig. 2: Links between investment and use costs

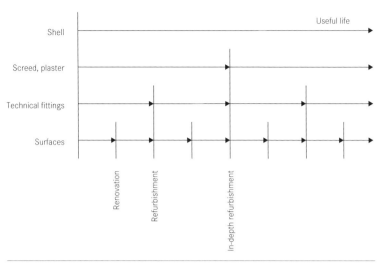

Fig. 3: Life cycle of building sections

Alongside the investment costs while a new building is under construction and the on-going maintenance costs, new investment is needed
at various intervals (maintenance and replacement costs) in the life cycle
of buildings in order to raise the structure to a more up-to-date technical
standard or to repair significant damage. Here a distinction is made
according to the part of the building concerned between various cycles
that may well turn out differently from project to project. The shell of the
building is generally the longest lasting section, and the end of its useful
life usually coincides with demolition and rebuilding. Sections with a robust finish such as the outer shell, plaster and screed are also pretty du-
rable and have to be replaced only after some decades. Technical fittings
(e.g. ventilation plants, plumbing, electrical installations, data systems
technology) and surfaces subject to wear and tear (e.g. paintwork, floor
coverings) last for a considerably shorter time and some of these are subject to very short investment cycles according to their function, construction method and maintenance level. > Fig. 3

This is why it is important to consider subsequent ease of replacement and the life cycles this implies at the planning stage. If technical features with short life cycles such as data cables or ventilation ducts
are installed underneath longer-lasting items (e.g. screed or plaster),
these will have to be removed and replaced as well during the procedure, along with all coverings and surfaces. This would mean that future

investment would be significantly more costly than would be the case if reversible and accessibly installed installations in a shaft were used, for example.

Generally speaking, clients will keep a careful eye on holding con- struction costs in check and – in the case of a longer-term interest in the use of the building – on their impact on the use phase as well. So architects and planners must accept that an interest in information and success are a central planning outcome and build the necessary working steps into the process. Keeping to budget and to the planned completion date are among the few physical known quantities that clients can and will use to judge the quality and professionalism of the architects and planners involved.

Basic budgeting principles

Some basic principles have to be set down at the outset if budgeting is to be understood. As well as defining the technical terms involved, it is above all necessary to ensure that the areas of influence and fluctuation range of building costs are grasped, as this is the basic essential for assessing the validity of costing. Handling imponderables and cost risks transparently is a key feature of responsible care for the client during the planning and construction process.

CONCEPTS AND STRUCTURES

Costs within the life cycle
If the entire life cycle of a building is considered, further use and disposal costs have to be taken into account alongside the actual construction costs. ISO 15686-5 defines life cycle costs (LCC) in the narrow sense as the sum of construction costs, running costs, cleaning and maintenance costs, and demolition or end of life costs. More broadly speaking, whole life costs (WLC) also include external costs not relating to construction, such as income, financing costs etc. > Fig. 4

Fixing the budget
A budget is fixed for almost all projects when the decision to put them in train is taken, regardless of whether it is a new building or an existing project, or whether a private or a public client is involved. The budget is not the same as the sum of money that provides the planning base for the work of architects and specialist planners. As a rule the budget contains additional cost factors for the client, e.g. plot acquisition, financing costs, additional internal costs, legal advice and solicitors' costs etc. Project related cost factors are relevant to the planning team ○ as a costing specification.

○ **Note:** A distinction has to be made between a costing specification as a fixed budget emanating from the client and the cost guarantee submitted by an architect. Here the architect is guaranteeing to keep within these costs and is thus liable for any additional costs that may be incurred – even if he or she is not responsible for generating them.

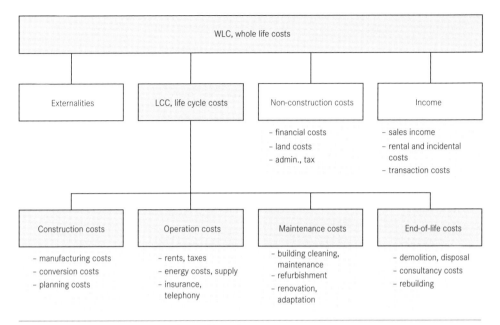

Fig. 4: Life cycle costs allocated according to ISO 15686-5

All subsequent costings in the planning and building process have to address this. A distinction has to be made between the maximum and the minimum principle when dealing with a costing specification.

Under the minimum principle, it is assumed that the client has fixed quality requirements and that these are to be realised at the lowest possible building costs. This applies, for example, when there are already fixed rental contracts in place, including building descriptions relating to later users, or if a hotel chain is building another hotel following a tried and tested, financially optimised scheme.

Minimum/maximum principle

The maximum principle works on the principle that that there is a fixed limit to costs, and that the greatest possible building volume and quality is be realised on this basis. This is the case for publicly funded housing, for example, where the maximum living space is to be realised within a fixed amount of funding. > Fig. 5

Budgeting is the generic term for all activities carried out during the planning and building process. Generally this includes listing costings,

Budgeting

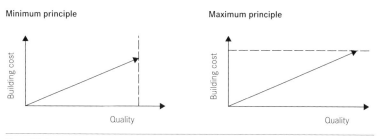

Fig. 5: Minimum and maximum principles

monitoring and checking results and events within the process, and also controlling activities such as feeding price increases into the budget.

Costings are prepared in stages in the course of the planning and building process, especially when the client has to make key decisions. For example, if it is necessary to decide whether a variant preliminary design should be pursued further or a planning proposal should be submitted to the authorities for approval, then the current cost position should be determined as a basis for the decision.

Two essential factors are involved in cost control. First, it means matching the current costings to the cost specifications and the previous costing stages, in order to be able to identify and evaluate any deviations from the process that may have occurred. Then the costs within the process have to be reviewed continuously, so that the client can be informed in good time about substantial cost-related consequences. This puts the client in a position from which it is possible to order direct measures such as quality adjustments or area reduction where necessary. Such interventions in the process are called cost control.

Cost classification   Another key factor is the way in which costs are presented and structured. Here a distinction is made between two fundamental ways of looking at things:

Cost classification based on structural components uses building systematics to structure the building costs that have been determined. Cost generating elements are listed according to the amount of detail required in terms of structural components (ceiling, wall, roof etc.) or by

Structural component bases	Building components	Contract award bases

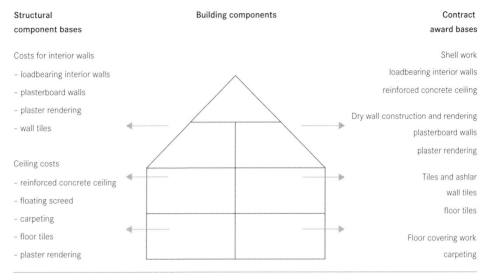

Structural component bases	Contract award bases
Costs for interior walls	Shell work
– loadbearing interior walls	loadbearing interior walls
– plasterboard walls	reinforced concrete ceiling
– plaster rendering	
– wall tiles	Dry wall construction and rendering
	plasterboard walls
	plaster rendering
Ceiling costs	
– reinforced concrete ceiling	Tiles and ashlar
– floating screed	wall tiles
– carpeting	floor tiles
– floor tiles	
– plaster rendering	Floor covering work
	carpeting

Fig. 6: Structural component-based and contract award-based

single structural elements (floor covering, screed, ceiling rendering etc.). Here the costs are fed into so-called cost groups. > Chapter on costing parameters

Cost classification based on award after tender is based on the subsequent structure of award units within the tendering and contract process. In this case, skills-related cost structures (shell, roof covering, screed, rendering, paintwork, electrical work etc.) are taken as the basis. > Chapter on working with a trade-oriented costing in the contract award phase

COSTING PARAMETERS

Building costs are calculated mainly by following a scheme of multiplying volumes/quantities within a costing parameter and then adding in individually identified costing parameters where appropriate. Here a distinction has to be made between various cost parameter types.

— Cubic capacity/plot area-related costing parameters
— Cost parameters for building components/raw elements (ceiling, roof, wall)
— Cost parameters for building components/light elements (ceiling rendering, reinforced concrete ceiling, screed, floor covering)
— Unit prices/tender prices (request for tenders or previously concluded projects)
— Construction estimate from contractors (personnel costs, material costs, site overheads)

Fig. 7: Specimen structural component based costing following German DIN 276

100 Plot	110 Plot value
	120 Additional plot costs
	130 Clearing
200 Preparation and access	210 Preparation
	220 Public access
	230 Private access
	240 Balancing charges
	250 Transitional charges
300 Building – building construction	310 Excavation
	320 Foundations
	330 Exterior walls
	340 Interior walls
	350 Ceilings
	360 Roofs
	370 Structural fittings
	390 Other building construction measures
400 Building – technical facilities	410 Sewerage, water and gas fittings
	420 Hot water facilities
	430 Ventilation facilities
	440 Electrical installations
	450 Telecom and IT facilities
	460 Conveyor systems
	470 Facilities for specified use
	480 Building automation
	490 Other technical equipment measures
500 Exterior work	510 Plot areas
	520 Reinforced areas
	530 Exterior buildings
	540 Technical facilities in external buildings
	550 Fixtures in external buildings
	560 Bodies of water
	570 Planted and seeded areas
	590 Other exterior facilities
600 Furnishings and artworks	610 Furnishings
	620 Artworks

700 Additional construction costs	710 Client requirements
	720 Preparation for property planning
	730 Architects' and engineers' fees
	740 Expert reports and consultation
	750 Artistic work
	760 Financing costs
	770 General additional construction costs
	790 Other additional construction costs

Volume- or area-related costings estimate the overall costs for a building by using parameters that are easily calculated from a design. In order to do this, the allotted overall sum required for a building and corresponding values such as

— gross cubic capacity (GCC) as the building volume
— gross floor area (GFA) as the sum of all the storey areas including construction areas or
— usable area (UA)

has to be established. Dividing these into each other gives rough values per square or cubic metre for future projects. Values of this kind often come in very useful in the early stages of a project, when no precise data, plans or quality requirements are available.

Volume- or area-related costings

One major problem when using volume- or area-related parameters arises because these do not relate to the actual cost factors. > Fig. 8

Cost generators ○

○ **Note:** A part of a building is known as a cost factor if it contributes to building costs in manufacture. $1\,m^2$ of reinforced concrete ceiling or $1\,m^2$ of masonry wall are direct cost factors, for example, but $1\,m^3$ of building volume or $1\,m^2$ of usable area generate costs only indirectly, because they all share proportionately in different cost factors. This inevitably involves conversion problems.

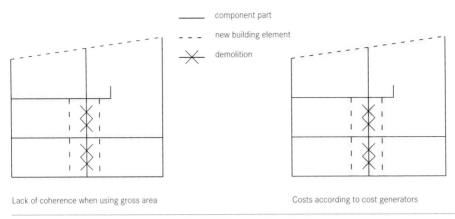

component part

new building element

demolition

Lack of coherence when using gross area   Costs according to cost generators

Fig. 8: Lack of precision in volume-/area-related building cost determination

Component- and
building elements   Parameters based on cost factors (building components, technical
facilities etc.) for a building are correspondingly more accurate. Com-
ponent-related parameters (also called component elements) sum up the
costs for a complete section of the building (ceiling price per m², roof
price per m²), and so are very simple to calculate after a superficial general survey of all parts of the building. Building-element related parameters (also called fine-element) allot a set quantity and a specific costing parameter to each individual structural element (m² of floor covering,
m² of screed, m² of reinforced concrete ceiling, m² of ceiling rendering,
m² of ceiling paintwork). This makes it possible to establish building costs
● much more precisely than with component elements.

● **Example:** The price for a component ceiling element
does not reveal anything at all about the individual
elements of the ceiling at first. But there are clear price
differences relating to ceiling construction (timber
beams, reinforced concrete) or floor coverings (natural
stone parquet, PVC covering etc.). This means that
existing prices must always be supported by additional
information and should not be applied to a particular project without embarking upon more elaborate
calculations.

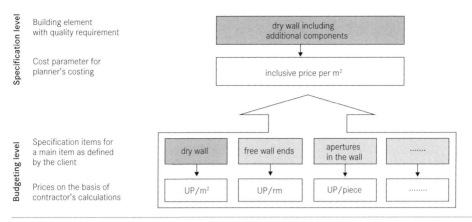

Fig. 9: Connection between building elements and unit prices (UP) in a tender

But building elements also include the whole range of typical additional components. So when setting a price per m² for floor coverings it must include skirting boards, connecting bars, penetrations etc., and a dry wall structure must include doorways, wall ends, connections etc. in the price per m². > Fig. 9

Inclusive price

Unit costs are the accounting prices offered by the contractor for each individual item in a tender. The unit cost in agreed contracts after precise calculation (not all-in contracts) forms the contractual basis between client and contractor. It is also possible to work out costs based on unit prices before the contract is awarded. This approach will be preceded by tenders backed up by statistically determined unit prices.

Unit cost

Unit prices offered by a building company will be determined in their turn on the basis of their single cost components. If costs as calculated by the contractor are used, this is known as an estimate. Estimating a tender for building work – regardless of whether it is based on an all-in price or a number of unit prices in a specification – is carried out according to business principles of cost and performance accounting. So a direct distinction is made between costs to be allocated to the work required and supplements for overheads or business expenses. > Fig. 10

Construction estimates

Costs that can be allocated directly are known as single partial service costs. These include wages, the cost of materials, equipment and machine costs and where applicable outside service costs that can be allotted to a service and are offered as an item for tender.

Individual partial service costs

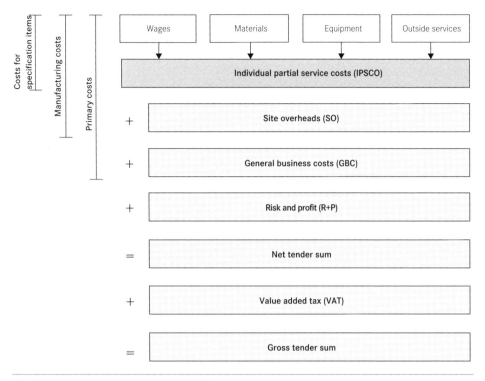

Fig. 10: Structural basis for a contractor estimate

The relevant wage elements within a unit costing are calculated from the average wage and the amount of time needed to produce one square metre of tiling, for example. The average wage includes social and additional wage costs, as well as the actual wage paid to employees. To calculate this, all the costs generated in a year for an employee are divided by the number of effective working hours per year (minus annual leave, sickness, training, public holidays etc.).

The relevant material costs within a unit costing include the purchase price for materials such as tiles, tile adhesive, and grouting cement for tiling, and also additional costs for breakages, waste etc. Auxiliary building materials (e.g. shuttering, supports) and fuel (e.g. fuel for a digger, power for a screed machine) are included in the calculation.

Outside service costs include all costs generated by sub-contractors such as hiring (of a mobile crane, for example, or a concrete pump) or separate contractors (e.g. sub-contracting for pointing by a dry builder).

Once all the above-mentioned costs that can be directly itemised Overheads and business expenses have been calculated, they are added to individual costs within the relevant section of the work. All items are additionally increased by supplements for further costs that may arise. These include building site overheads, general business costs and supplements for risk/profit.

Building site overheads (BSO) include all costs that cannot be allocated directly to the building work but that are nevertheless generated within the building operation. This includes items such as accommodation expenses, site insurance, expenses on the contractors' management side etc.

General business costs (GBC) are the building contractors' non-operative running costs that that have to be covered proportionately across all building sites. These include office rental and upkeep, for example, management salaries, upkeep and security for a builders' yard, and costs for legal and tax advice.

Finally, risk and profit (R+P) represent the commercial result that the building project would like to achieve, over and above the previous prime costs.

Generally speaking, such different levels of detail can be graded from volume-/area-related cost parameters down to detailed business cost elements in the contractors' budgeting. Appropriate parameters are used as a basis according to the costing methods chosen. > Chapter on costing methods

COST PREDICTION PRINCIPLES

The point in time at which costings are made is called the cost estimation point. Cost estimation point It is possible for there to be some years between the cost estimates made in the early planning phases and the award of the building contract or the final costing for the building work as charged. This makes it difficult to predict future market price changes and include them in the costing.

So in fact costing can be based only on the conditions prevailing at the time, as future developments are speculative and thus of little relevance. But it is important for the client to know how much money will ultimately have to be paid for a project.

The following actions can be taken to reduce this difference:
— Assess and estimate possible variables in future cost movements.
  > Chapter on influences on costs

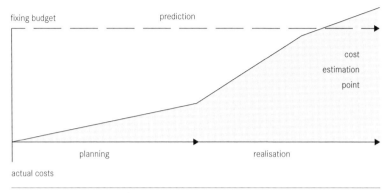

fixing budget   prediction

cost
estimation
point

planning   realisation

actual costs

Fig. 11: Cost prediction principle

— Carry out the best possible risk investigations. > Chapter on assessing
    cost risks
— Do not see costing as static but update it throughout the whole
    process and keep adjusting it to current developments. > Chapter on
    updating the budget

FACTORS INFLUENCING COSTS

If building costs are to be estimated purposefully and realistically it
is essential to understand the connection between planning qualities and
costs as well as going through a technical costing exercise. Costing
parameters are available for all the levels presented in the chapter on
costing parameters via statistical listings, online platforms or books. But
only the architect responsible can adapt them to suit a particular project.

General influences that may well make the project in question different from your own have to be taken into account, particularly in the
case of parameters that are not directly linked to cost factors. > Fig. 12

Scale and context   The scale of a project is highly relevant to the costs per square
metre, as small projects are often associated proportionately with higher
expenditure.

If very difficult sites are involved such as an inner city area that has
to be developed in its entirety, then it will be extremely difficult and
expensive to organise the building site, as it may be that external areas

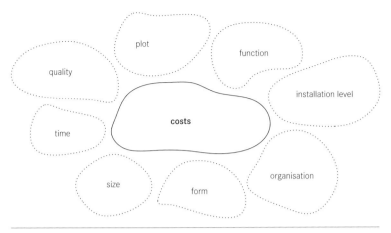

Fig. 12: Factors influencing building costs

will have to be rented and streets closed, which will cost money. If the site is not accessible by a developed road (e.g. a research observatory in a high mountain range), then considerable expenses may well be generated in getting to the building site.

●

It is goes without saying that different buildings such as dwellings, offices, warehouses or laboratories cannot be compared in terms of volume- or area-related parameters, because the installations required and the complexity of the projects can differ considerably. Building costs depend on the technical installations, particularly for projects needing large quantities of domestic installations. So if volume- and area-related parameters are being applied, then a building with a similar function should be used for comparison.

Function and complexity

If the project for which estimates are to be prepared is within the existing building stock and is to be converted or refurbished, considerably greater costs will be involved than for a new building. In the sphere

Projects in existing building stock

● **Example:** If we consider the degree of site preparation and clearing needed to lay screed, this will depend on whether a medium-sized building is to be treated, or just a single room. If calculated by the square metre price for the screed, the relevant building overheads will be significantly higher in the case of a very small project.

of monument preservation, individual finishing and adjustment work is often necessary, with large numbers of personnel involved. Many building contractors work on the basis of higher expenditure simply because the project in question deals with existing building stock. They know from experience that wide-ranging problems and special features will mean that it will not be possible to work as efficiently as for a new building.

Building period The building period required for a project can also be very important if building has to be carried out very quickly or will be subject to a large number of interruptions. If the contractor can use employees only for short periods – for example because breaks have to be taken in the course of work on projects in existing building stock that continue to be in use – s/he will also have to factor in wage costs for the unproductive intermediate periods. If realisation times are very short, additional costs for personnel and machines will have to be built in. The provision of building site facilities can also be a key factor in terms of overall costs, especially if these costs are not reflected in the physical end result – the fabric of the building.

Quality The quality of both architecture and the materials is significant in the same way. Products made mechanically in large production runs offer considerable savings over components made by hand. Material prices can rise exponentially in the luxury sector, for example for kitchens, bathroom furniture, tiles, facades etc. In the case of individually designed and produced components such as special facade structures or windows it may be necessary to take further expenses into account, such as individual permits and technical experts, as well as individual manufacturing costs.

Wages and material costs Generally speaking, the question arises of the extent to which producing a construction element is very labour-intensive and thus dominated by wage costs, or whether its key features are rapid installation and possibly high material costs. In countries with high wage levels it is preferable to opt for industrial prefabrication and simple delivery/installation instead of craft work and raw materials processed on site.

If the component being budgeted for is a work-intensive construction element, changing wage costs may be relevant for price increases in the planning and building process. Additional wage costs may have to be taken into account, as well as general wage scale variations. And some materials may vary considerably in cost as a result of fluctuating raw material prices. Metal prices in particular (e.g. for steel girders, reinforcement or electric cables) are very heavily dependent on world demand, particularly from China, India and other rapidly developing markets.

But regional and local market fluctuations have to be taken into account, as well as world trade and international raw material prices. If the building trade is doing well in the economic cycle and building contractors have full order books, prices will be much higher than in times of underemployment when every contractor is desperate for orders. Sometimes prices can fluctuate by 20–30% between recession and growth phases.

Market prices/ economic developments

ASSESSING COST RISKS

The above explanations make it clear that it is sensible or even essential to conduct a risk assessment operation. It needs to be said from the outset that the concept of "risk" should not be seen as negative in the broader sense. In comparison with "security", a risk means first and foremost a lack of knowledge about the state of affairs or uncertainty about whether something is going to happen.

Risks cannot usually be excluded, but simply confined or minimised. Expense incurred in doing this (e.g. general site or contamination tests) are known as due diligence. So a decision has to be made about which costs make sense within a project, so that potentially damaging effects can be kept to a minimum. > Fig. 13

Risks in the broader sense are fundamentally assessed on the basis of the incidence rate and the damaging effect in each case. In particular, the risks that are very damaging with disastrous consequences and are very likely to occur have to be limited in advance. The rigour of the examination and the limits to due diligence are fixed for individual projects. It can be helpful to limit risk to a tolerable and above all financially viable level by using the ALARP method (As Low As Reasonably Practicable). > Fig. 14

Damaging effects and the incidence rate

Cost risks can be allotted in terms of their origin in various risk areas. As has already been explained, market risks such as fluctuations in the economic cycle can lead to considerable budget changes. Business risks

Market and commercial risks

● **Example:** A few decades ago, attics were still made by carpenters from rough timbers, but now CAD drawings are used to prepare all the necessary purlins and rafters ready for fitting in the factory, using joinery machines. Even though some of the machines are very costly, they are considerably more cost-efficient than hand production.

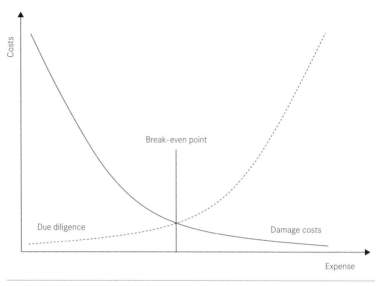

Fig. 13: Connections between damage costs and due diligence

such as strikes or insolvency also represent a high uncertainty factor for the success of the project.

Subsoil risks   Subsoil risks also have to be taken into account. For example, high groundwater levels can require elaborate reinforcement in the cellar and temporary lowering of groundwater levels in the building phase. If the subsoil turns out during the building phase to be non-loadbearing, compensatory measures (pile foundations, soil improvement, anchoring, load distribution slabs etc.), which are usually elaborate and very cost intensive, have to be undertaken.

Risk in existing
building stock   Particular risks in existing building stock have to be taken into account for projects in existing stock. These can include:
— contamination (asbestos, PCB, PAH, AMF, timber protection agents etc.)
— static stability can no longer be guaranteed (non-existent documentation, corrosion, inappropriate interventions etc.)
— data unavailable (missing plans/planning permission for the project, unapproved modifications, building geometry etc.)
— damage to parts of building (damp penetration, mould formation, cracks etc.)

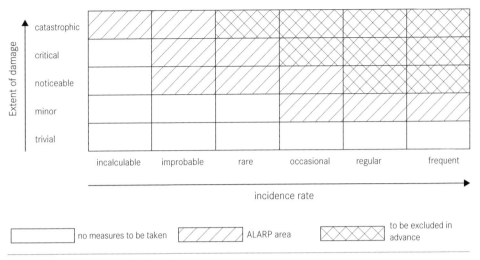

Fig. 14: Riskograph using the ALARP method

— preservation measures not addressed (adaptation to current regulations needed)
— domestic services (ramshackle piping, lack of spare parts, adaptation to current regulations etc.)
— fire protection requirements (upgrading, compensatory measures, replacement etc.)
— and so on

This is why is it necessary to assess the building land and any existing building where appropriate carefully at the beginning of the project, in order to minimise the greatest of these risks.

Major uncertainties in terms of keeping within the costs as fixed frequently arise as a result of setting the project budget early and on the basis of insufficient data. Fluctuation in the area- or volume-related parameters arise because no reference has been made to cost factors as described above, and in addition to this qualities are often described imprecisely in the early stages, e.g. "average quality", which leaves considerable scope for interpretation.

Costing risks

Fig. 15: Example of a risk assessment

Risk	Cost	Effect/ consequence	Percentage risk	Risk costs
Building permission not granted	EUR 70,000	End of project due and previous planning	30%	EUR 21,000
Subsoil not loadbearing	EUR 40,000	Ground improvement needed	25%	EUR 10,000
Steel price rises	EUR 80,000	Tender prices have to be adjusted	10%	EUR 8,000
Shell contractor declared insolvent	EUR 250,000	Increased price as a result of delay and new contractor	3%	EUR 7,500
...	...	...	...	...

Risk assessment methods

The first key basis for assessing cost risks involves addressing possible risk areas. While it is possible to reduce uncertainty through early analysis and expert reports, risks cannot be definitely ruled out until completion and the final invoice. So possible risks areas have to be recorded from the outset, assessed in terms of damage caused and the incidence rate, and then observed throughout the process and the assessment updated in order to guarantee complete risk management. As this involves considerable effort and expense, risk must be assessed in direct relation to the project and an agreement reached about the level of detail and assessment to be taken as a basis.

Now usually only a few potential dangers actually emerge during the planning and building process, so it is not very helpful just to add up the possible risk costs. So the risk budget can be assessed using various mathematical processes, but this depends to a very large extent on the client's risk awareness. One possibility is to present the risks using the following formula:

$$\text{Risk budget} = \sqrt{C_{\text{Risk 1}}{}^2 + C_{\text{Risk 2}}{}^2 + C_{\text{Risk 3}}{}^2 + \ldots}$$

Risk buffer

One typical approach in dealing with costs risks is to build in a risk buffer. This can be placed in the costing as a cost item or planning in optionally as a possibly quality reduction. > Fig. 16

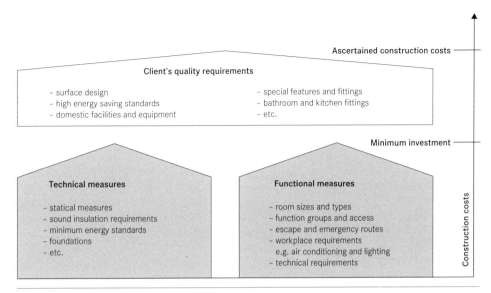

Fig. 16: Buffering cost fluctuations

In this way, modules are identified that can be used for buffering should a risk occur. These are usually based on finishing requirements for the later stages of the project such as floor coverings, external facilities etc. Essential basic requirements for this method are:

— the client's agreement
— the cost relevance of the selected construction elements
  (for example, the quality of the toilet walls offers only a very small buffer in a EUR 20 million project)
— that the contract has not yet been awarded (if parts of an agreed building contract are cancelled, further payments still have to be made to the building contractor)

Unforeseen costs can be dealt with by, for example, building in phases, fixing optional building stages (e.g. developing the attic storey), keeping alternatives open in the case of major cost factors (PVC floors, granite floors etc.). The saving potential of these buffers has to be calculated and a final date set for when each option within the process is freely available. > Fig. 17

Fig. 17: Example of modular risk buffering

Cost module	Overall module cost	Saving potential	Available until
Addition of two garages and possibly carport	EUR 18,000	EUR 15,000	March 2014
Extending attic storey, possibly only insulating ceiling	EUR 30,000	EUR 12,000	July 2014
Ashlar floor covering, or linoleum	EUR 25,000	EUR 12,000	August 2014
Exterior garden development, or possibly only grass	EUR 50,000	EUR 20,000	November 2014

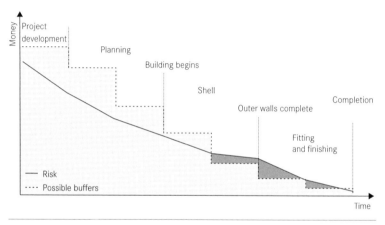

Fig. 18: Risks and buffers compared

Risks and their financial implications, and their savings potential, can be compared directly in this way, and related to a timescale. This also shows up corresponding gaps in cover provision. > Fig. 18

Costing methods

There are various ways of drawing up costings. The choice of method depends on the project phase concerned or the depth of planning achieved. The fundamental principle is that costing figures are always multiplied by a unit of quantity in order to be able to make a statement about the costs to be expected. > Chapter on costings For example, the more detailed the available information about the quality of wall and floor surfaces or technical domestic equipment standards, the more precisely this can be taken into account when costings are being drawn up. There is usually not much available in terms of detailed information at the beginning of a project, as this has still to be established in agreement with the client or the various specialist planners in the course of the planning process. But the amount and type of space needed is usually fixed from the outset, as this is clear from the intended use or from the prescribed spatial programme, which means that appropriate cubic capacity and floor areas can be worked out and costs calculated. The more details about the planned building are fixed, the more possible it should be to produce detailed costings. The various costing methods and their application potential for various project phases are described below.

COSTING BASED ON CUBIC CAPACITY

One costing possibility in the very early stages of a project is to calculate the cubic capacity of the building and to multiply it by a cost figure.

Cubic capacity is derived from the area of the building and its height from the foundation of the floor slab to the top edge of the roof covering. In Germany, cubic capacity parameters are defined precisely in DIN 277, which calculates them as gross cubic capacity (GCC). Costing figures can be obtained from national building cost information services (> Literature chapter), who record and evaluate these statistically by project type, finishing standard and use. > Fig. 20 It is also possible for individuals to devise or set up their own costing systems, provided that a large number of projects of the same type, similar size and finishing standard have been planned, built and budgeted for. In such cases the building costs are finally worked out at the end of the project and then calculated back to the cubic capacity of the building as a rough reference unit. It is essential to ensure that uniform references are made to cost values and quantities. Construction costs calculated from the cubature of the building always remain imprecise, as it is necessary to rely on very rough assumptions about construction quality and to an extent about quantities as well, and it may well be that no definitive building design is available. Direct

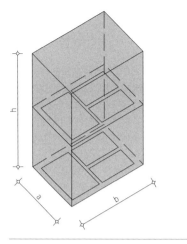

Fig. 19: Calculating the gross cubic capacity

links with cost factors are also not available. > Chapter on costings So working out the expected building costs based on gross cubic capacity is simply a planning instrument for defining building targets in terms of quantity and quality.

If the gross cubic capacity needed for a building project has already been fixed, it is then possible to check the essential feasibility or financial viability of a construction project by using product-specific cost figures. Following the minimum principle > Chapter on concepts and structures, the quantities here are provided by the gross cubic capacity and the qualities by the choice of the project-specific cost figure. But by the client can follow the maximum principle and name a certain sum for construction expenses as the target cost specification, which will then make it possible to aim for the maximum building size that can be achieved and / or the best possible qualities and finish characteristics within the costs as fixed.

Example 1:
Specifying the gross
cubic capacity
An investor wants to erect a new office building. The gross cubic capacity is laid down by the maximum size of building allowed on the plots, which is 3000 m³. The investor provides the architect with rough information about the desired standard of finish and the material quality of the building. But as no definite plans have yet been made for the office building, the architect can draw up a costing only on the basis of the information provided by the investor. The architect has no costings of his or her own derived from similar buildings, and so turns to a information service to find a comparable property that is closest to the design ideas and the requirements for the new building. > Fig. 20

Fig. 20: Costings for average standard office and HQ buildings

Office and HQ buildings, average standard
Costings for building construction and technical features and fittings
15 properties for comparison of 30, see property information
GCC of 2,200 m³ to 29,000 m³, GFA of 780 m² to 9,500 m², UA of 580 m² to 7,500 m²

Reference unit	Lower value	Average value	Higher value
GCC	EUR 300/m³	**EUR 375/m³**	EUR 475/m³
GFA	EUR 1250/m²	**EUR 1500/m²**	EUR 1750/m²
UA	EUR 2000/m²	**EUR 2500/m²**	EUR 3000/m²

It is usual to give certain price ranges (from ... to ...) for the cost parameters. If no further clear and detailed information about the building is available it is advisable to use the average cost figures at first and make the client aware of the fluctuation ranges by means of additions and deductions.

Gross cubic capacity × costing = building costs to be expected
3,000 m³ × EUR 375/m³ = EUR 1,125,000

The given cost figures actually lie between EUR 3000/m³ and EUR 475/m³. So the fluctuation is moves between EUR 225,000 downwards and EUR 200,000 upwards.

An investor lays down a fixed investment sum of EUR 800,000 for a new office building. As he wants to let the building later, he wants the architect to provide some information about the maximum built area he can aim to achieve. Costings can be researched via standards fixed as in example 1, and this means that details about the gross cubic capacity that can be realised can also be obtained. The following calculation does not represent an actual costing, but is an important planning instrument in the early project phase.

Example 2:
Specifying the
construction costs

The GCC that can be realised for the office building is estimated as follows:

Fixed investment sum: cost value =
possible gross cubic capacity
EUR 800 000: EUR 375/m³ = approx. 2133 m³

The architect should inform the investor about corresponding consequences for the gross cubic capacity that can be realised on the basis of the costs, which extend from EUR 300/m³ to EUR 475/m³ > Fig. 20. So

○ **Note:** Once the gross cubic capacity that can be realised is established it is possible, by using conversion
factors for the storey heights (incl. structures on floors
and ceilings), to calculate the gross area and build it
into the preliminary design for the building as a planning requirement. A further calculation based on the
net floor area of the building and deductions for necessary additional areas can also lead to a statement
about the rentable space that can be realised without a
definite preliminary design for the building

the fluctuation range for the estimated possible gross cubic capacity is
between approx. 2,666 m³ and 1,684 m³.

Example 3:
Specifying the gross
cubic capacity and
the building costs It is not unusual for the client to prescribe both the desired cubic
capacity and also a fixed budget for the building costs to the architect. If
this is the case, a costing can be calculated by dividing the target costs
by the desired cubic capacity, and this will give some insight into the qual-
○ ity that can be achieved or whether the project can be realised at all.

The client would like to erect an office building with a gross cubic
capacity of 3,500 m³ for EUR 800,000. The following equation makes it
possible to calculate a project-specific costing.

Fixed investment sum:
gross cubic capacity = costing
EUR 800,000: 3500 m³ = approx. EUR 228/m³

Now the architect has to set the calculated cost against the other
properties available for comparison in order to check whether the client's
ideas can be realised at all. The lowest cost for comparable office buildings is EUR 300/m³ of gross cubic capacity. > Fig. 20 If the calculated cost
falls within the price fluctuations for the comparable properties, the building project can definitely be realised in the form desired. If, as in the sample quotation, the calculated cost falls clearly below that of the comparable properties, then the architect's targets are questionable. In this
case the architect and the client can decide whether to concentrate on
keeping to the target costs or to the desired gross cubic capacity, as it
seems that the project cannot be realised within the target costs. If the
desired gross cubic capacity still has to be achieved, the target costs will
have to be corrected upwards. If the client is prepared to scale the project down, the architect can follow example 1 and use a realistic costing
○ to calculate the gross cubic capacity that can be realised.

Calculating construction costs by using the cubic capacity of a building, as shown in the examples, is a very flexible planning instrument for
early project phases without a definitive building design. But the results
must always be treated critically, and system-related fluctuations should
definitely be pointed out.

Typical imponderables for this method are:

Information provided by participating specialist planners or local authorities can greatly influence costs at the later stages of the project, and
these are often not predictable in the early stages. Alongside costing fluctuations and unclear definitions of the desired qualities for the standard
of finish, changing the storey heights that have been accepted can have
a great influence on the building costs as calculated. Changed ceiling or
floor heights can influence the gross cubic capacity. It can be necessary,
according to how high the standard for the technical installations in a
building is to be (bus system, ventilation plant etc.), for additional installation levels such as double floors and false ceilings to be required. This
means that, given a planned clear room height of 3.00 m, the necessary
storey height can easily vary between 3.40 and 4.50 m. Without using a
specialist planner who can undertake to set the dimensions for the installation levels, it is not possible to settle the actual storey heights, and
thus the height of the building, finally in the early project phases. But this
considerably affects building costs.

On the other hand, increasing the gross cubic capacity does not have
to go hand in hand with a catastrophic increase in costs.

For a factory hall (e.g. with dimensions of 20 m × 80 m × 9 m), increasing the height of the building by a metre affects the building costs less,
as the cost factors for the foundations or floor slab and the roof structure remain the same, and only the facade area is increased by 200 m².
> Fig. 21 So in the building itself it is essentially only the adapted "air space"
that becomes larger, but this cannot be seen as increasing the cost.

○ **Note:** The costings for gross cubic capacity should not be calculated from an average value for a typical building typology alone. If an office building is being planned, for example, information from building cost information services will usually list several properties for reference, differing in size and design. Here the architect should use the costs for the building project that he or she feels most closely resembles his/her own. Information about individual properties for comparison can be taken from the property details. Given inadequate links with the actual cost factors at the building elements level, the correct choice of property for comparison is the only way of keeping any state-ment about costs as realistic as possible.

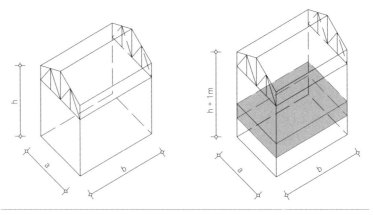

Fig. 21: Factory halls with the same area and different gross cubic capacity

COSTING BASED ON FLOOR AREA AND USABLE AREA

Another way of calculating construction costs involves calculating the floor area or usable area and multiplying that by a relevant cost figure. Here the height of the building is more or less ignored. This makes it all the more important to use costings for comparable properties with similar absolute storey heights (including structural superstructure for foundations, intermediate floors and roofs). In the same way, costing based on floor area and usable area is of only limited usefulness for working out reliable or robust statements about the costs that can actually be anticipated, given that here – as is also the case for calculation based on gross cubic capacity – there is no direct link with the cost factors. It is best to see this costing method in combination with costing based on gross cubic capacity and building- or use-specific conversion factors as a planning instrument for the early phases of the project. In any case it is advisable to compare the results from the volume- and area-related costing methods, as in this way the results can be checked and it becomes possible to aim for a realistic approximation to the actual building costs. Costing based on floor area and usable area is explained with examples.

Costing based on
gross floor area

Determining the expected construction costs based on the gross floor area uses similarly simple calculation methods to those used previously for gross cubic capacity.

As has been pointed out already, there is no direct connection between costing figures and the actual cost factors. Factors contributing

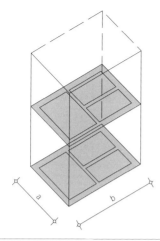
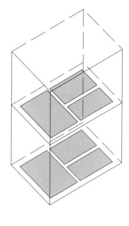

Fig. 22: Calculating floor area and usable area

to increased costs such as additional lift equipment, for example, additional staircase cores providing for shorter routes through the building or especially high ceiling and floor superstructures that are required because the standard of the technical fittings has been raised are not considered separately. As is also the case for the gross cubic capacity method, the costings for gross floor areas can be included in the construction cost planning in a variety of ways.

Here the following possible approaches can be used:
1. The necessary gross floor area is laid down directly by the client or the gross floor area that can be realised on the plot is established and the construction costs are calculated by multiplying them by the costs.

2. The client sets a prescribed target cost. The gross floor area that can be realised within the cost framework is calculated by dividing the target costs by an appropriate cost figure (taking the desired qualities into account).

An investor intends to put up an office building with a gross floor area of 3000 m². He asks the architect to estimate the building costs entailed so that he can raise the finance. The architect researches costings for comparable properties intended for the same use and of the same size (obtaining this information from construction cost enquiry services or from his own experience of such costing), and is thus able to prepare a first rough statement about the building costs. An average price of

Example 1:
Specifying the gross
floor area

EUR 1,500/m² GFA is to provide the basis for the calculation, and subsequent fluctuations with additions and deductions are to be considered when estimating the costs. > Fig. 20

Gross floor area × costing figure =
expected building costs
3500 m² × EUR 1500/m³ = EUR 4,500,000

The result of the calculation comes out at EUR 4,500,000 and can deviate up or down by up to EUR 750,000 in each case on the basis of the costings referenced.

But if the client specifies terms based on target costs or the gross floor area and the target costs, simple calculation methods as in examples 2 and 3 can be used based on the gross cubic capacity.

Calculation based on the usable area   The calculation of construction costs based on the gross floor area of a building, as described above, is very easy for the architect to use, and also readily comprehensible. But most clients are not property experts, and so can make relatively little of planning costs calculated in this way. In the case of private housing construction and rented office property the areas that can be actually used or let are placed in the foreground, as it is based on these that later use or later income and profit can be determined. A cost estimate relating to the usable area (UA) will be more accessible to the client as he is familiar with his actual use-specific area requirements from his own experience, and can thus evaluate a project better in terms of economic viability in this way. The client can give the architect specifications for the usable area relatively easily by referring to previous area requirements and any increase that is necessary for the future. But it is not unusual for much more abstract specifications to be given, based for example on the necessary number of employees laid down by a company (e.g. at least 1500 employees in single offices), the number of beds required in a hotel, or on a particular number of single or double rooms in hospitals.

■ **Tip:** In any costing, the upper and lower values should be listed in the calculation, so that system-related fluctuation ranges in the costing method can be seen. If the architect provides the client with nothing but a single figure for the possible construction costs, that figure is made to seem unduly significant.

If, as mentioned above, the client gives the architect much more abstract specifications, then the architect must establish the area needed in each case and the usable area required for this, as this is the parameter that is relevant for his construction planning. Construction costs calculated by reference to area or cubic capacity can then be recalculated retrospectively to relate to project-specific abstract reference factors, so that the client can always keep an eye on this in the contexts of financial viability checks. Area requirements and conversion calculations made in relation to particular reference points should always be worked out in close agreement with the client.

A client intends to erect an office building for 600 employees. As well as individual offices for the employees, the client says that, exactly as in his present office building, approx. 400 m² of additional area is required for toilets, corridors, foyer, kitchens, storage etc., and a further four conference rooms each of 60 m². The architect works on the basis of simple cubicle offices, each with an area of 14 m². Given the same economical use of space as in the present building and the additional conference rooms required in the new building, the following calculation for the usable area emerges:

Example 1: Specifying the number of employees

Area required/employees × number of employees +
additional area required = usable area
$14 \text{ m}^2 \times 600 + 400 \text{ m}^2 + (4 \times 60 \text{ m}^2) = 9040 \text{ m}^2$

Costings for comparable properties come out between EUR 2000/m² and EUR 3000/m² usable area (average value EUR 2500/m²). > Fig. 20

The expected building costs are calculated as follows:

usable area × costing figure = expected building costs
$9040 \text{ m}^2 \times \text{EUR } 2500/\text{m}^2 = \text{EUR } 22,600,000$

Regarding the expected building costs, a fluctuation range of EUR 4,520,000 upwards and downwards should be allowed for.

Costing based on the gross floor area of a building is as quick and easy to use as calculation based on gross cubic capacity, but it is equally imprecise. If the usable area required is specified by the client or worked out by the architect, corresponding cost figures can be taken as a basis. But then a decision has to be made when selecting the cost figures about whether similarly economical use of space is possible for this particular project. If the ground plan arrangement and access facilities were to differ significantly, this would create problems in relation to the building costs as calculated. This is why it is particularly important to select

Advantages and disadvantages of costing based on floor area and usable area

comparable properties correctly. It is also necessary to decide to what extent additional floor space can or may be calculated into the usable area, or the area that can be let out subsequently. Failure to take account of the height of the building when using this method can lead to further imprecision in the case of non-standard storey heights. As almost every building client finds usable area a comprehensible and familiar parameter, it offers the best way of checking specifications and requests, and makes costs readily intelligible. Calculating the building costs to be expected by reference to the usable area can make the result noticeably more precise if applied correctly, as the costing parameters take further information about the financial viability of the space into account. But this concealed information about the financial viability of the space can also bring great imprecision in its wake if no reference objects with appropriately realistic cost parameters are available for concrete comparison, or the depth of planning achieved for the project so far does not make it possible to say anything on this.

COSTING BASED ON COMPONENT ELEMENTS

No reference is made in the above-mentioned calculation methods to the actual cost factors. In the early project phases it is a matter of checking feasibility within a certain cost framework, defining the contract range and developing a building design that conforms to these conditions.

But these rough calculation methods are too imprecise for the later planning stages, which means that a more detailed calculation method is needed. One option here is to calculate the building costs in terms of component elements. But a definitive building design is essential for this, as quantities have to be calculated for the individual structural building components (component elements) needed for the planned building. A uniform procedure must be followed when establishing quantities for the individual component elements. A component element applies to individual parts of the building such as an exterior wall, for example, a ceiling or a roof, and it can be further broken down into construction elements.

○ **Note:** Basically, the ratio of the usable area to the gross floor area expresses the financial viability of the space. The fewer the construction and traffic areas needed for the same gross floor area, the more economical the building will be.

■ **Tip:** It is rare for a building to use the same component elements all the time. This is why it is necessary to distinguish between possible ceiling, wall and roof structures clearly at an early stage when working out the building costs, as this considerably increases the accuracy of the costing, while only relatively unreliable costing statements can be made without reliable information about the composition of the individual component parts.

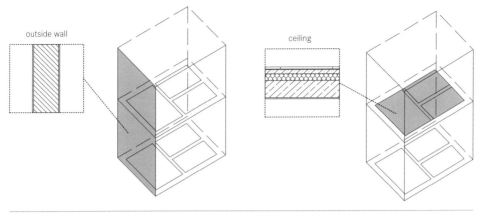

outside wall

ceiling

Fig. 23: Outside wall and ceiling as component element

For example, a ceiling as a component element can be made up as follows:

1. tiles, d = 15 mm + adhesive
2. floating cement screed 6.0 cm
3. thermal insulation, footfall sound insulation 5.0 cm
4. reinforced concrete ceiling 25 cm
5. ceiling plaster rendering 1.5 cm
6. paint

The architect proceeds as follows when calculating the building costs to be expected:

The existing design for the building is evaluated by reference to its individual structural components. A table is made of the individual component elements and they are described in more detail if possible. Then quantities are worked out separately for each component element and also entered in the table. > Fig. 24 It is possible to use the individual component element descriptions to research appropriately comparable costings through building cost information services, or to use parameters drawn up by the architect or planner. These cost figures now relate to a specific part of the building, rather than simply to a building type. This creates a direct connection between cost factors and cost figures. As well as this, cost figures from various objects for comparison can be cited, as comparability is evaluated by reference to the structural addition. The costings for the individual component elements are multiplied by the established quantities, giving a total for the individual group of component elements (roof, outside wall, inside wall, ceiling, foundations). If individual components are omitted from the quantity survey, this will have a considerable effect on the building costs as calculated. ■

Fig. 24: Example of a simple costing using component elements allocated to cost groups according to German standard DIN 276.

DIN 276 cost group	Description of component	Quantity, unit of quantity	Cost EUR/unit	Total price in EUR
310	Excavation pit	900 m³	8	7,200
320	Foundations	120 m²	150	18,000
330	Outside walls	200 m²	300	60,000
340	Inside walls	80 m²	150	12,000
350	Ceilings	120 m²	165	19,800
360	Roofs	120 m²	220	26,400
......	....	....	......	....
Total building costs				**230,800**

Advantages and disadvantages of costing based on component elements

Costing based on component elements makes it possible to work out the costs by reference to the cost factors, and is thus considerably more precise than calculation methods using building volumes or areas. But it is difficult to reduce the component elements to a single structural item in each case. The calculation will take a lot more time if the component elements are described and recorded in a sophisticated way, taking all the different structural elements into account. But as has already been pointed out, surface finishes, which affect the cost of a component element significantly, are not specified until much later. Precise building costs can be worked out very quickly and in a very uncomplicated way for very simple buildings with few different structural features. But if a building is planned in a way that is highly individual, technical and architecturally ambitious, calculation by component elements can result in a high potential for imprecision. Like the above-mentioned costing methods, building projects in existing stock are very difficult to illustrate or cost using component elements. A further problem lies in the fact that different specialist areas or craftsmen doing the work are mixed up together when costing for a component element.

The list below shows which skilled workers are already involved in the above-mentioned example of the ceiling:

1. Tiling and slab-work for the floor covering (33%)
2./3. Screed work for the screed including insulation (13%)
4. Concrete and reinforced concrete for the loadbearing ceiling (44%)
5. Rendering and stucco for the interior ceiling rendering (7%)
6. Painting and decorating for the ceiling rendering (3%)

The following skilled work can be needed for an outside wall as a component element:

1. Masonry for the outside wall (65%)
2. Rendering and stucco work for the interior and exterior rendering (27%)
3. Painting and decorating for the facade and for painting the interior wall rendering (8%)

As can be seen from the two examples of component elements for a ceiling and an outside wall, factoring the estimated construction costs into the budget for the individual tendering units is a very fiddly procedure when the project later moves from the planning to the realisation stage. > Chapter on work with a skilled-trade oriented costing This is achieved by breaking down the percentage costs of a component element to relate to the individual skills involved. But this approach is questionable, as the percentage cost is very strongly affected by project-specific conditions in the objects chosen for comparison.

COSTING BASED ON CONSTRUCTION ELEMENTS

Costing with the aid of component elements does indeed offer the possibility of working out the building costs based on cost generators, but it leads to imprecision and to problems of application as the project runs its course. This is why a more precise breakdown of the costs, down to the individual construction elements, should be carried out as soon as sufficiently precise information is available about planned structural additions and surface qualities. > Chapter on working with component-oriented costing approaches

Before costing based on construction elements is explained, the concept of a "construction element" should be unambiguously defined. A building element can also be called a fine element, a component, a structural component etc., but these terms cannot be precisely defined. The following explanation is unambiguous: a construction element is a part of a building that can be designated as a component and also assigned to a particular construction skill.

All component elements in a building can be subdivided into individual building elements. An outside wall and a ceiling are shown as examples of component elements in figure 25.

This costing method is based on a building description, which must contain all the construction elements in the planned building. Different costings can be assigned to the individual building elements on the basis

○ **Note:** This means that a construction element cannot be subdivided further according to its function in the building (e.g. a "wall, non-loadbearing or load-bearing, including doors" can be subdivided into non-loadbearing walls, loadbearing walls, and doors). There are no construction elements that can be assigned to several work areas or tender units – for example, "ceiling plaster with emulsion paint" can be subdivided as construction element one "ceiling plaster, rendering work" and construction element two "emulsion paint, painting and decorating".

○ **Note:** In the case of a dry construction wall, for example, it is important to have information about the thickness of the wall, details about the materials required for insulation, and also the materials and the thickness required for the planking layers, as this will imply certain fire- and sound-insulation require-ments that make a crucial impact on the costs. If a wall consists of two separately constructed partition walls, this also affects costs considerably, as it increases the amount of time needed for the work, and thus the wages to be paid for doing it.

of the qualities as described. As each construction element is defined unambiguously, the costings used for comparison can also be selected very realistically. This construction element catalogue presents all the construction elements in the building in tabular form. In contrast with a room schedule, all the construction elements that are structurally the same are described only once, so that even for large projects the total quantity falls within a manageable framework that is easy to handle. The description should restrict itself to the essential characteristics needed to distinguish between different qualities. But the construction elements must be listed in full, in order to guarantee a precise result for the cost-ing that will be determined later.

Procedure   When drawing up the construction element catalogue, the architect goes through the individual cost groups for a building and notes all the relevant construction elements. For example, all the non-loadbearing interior walls are listed and described briefly, along with their qualities and requirements. The same is done for all the other construction ele-ments, such as loadbearing interior walls, loadbearing exterior walls, exterior wall cladding etc. The services required (skill areas needed for the work) should also be identified in this table, not just the cost groups, so that the calculated building costs for individual construction elements can be collated in order to create budgets for the tendering units. In this way, it is easy at any time to move from a building- to a realisation-oriented view within table calculation software. The specified services for the later tender units can be also be summed up project-specifically
○   according to the range of services offered by the contracting firms.

Allocation by rooms   It makes complete sense to identify rooms in the construction ele-ment catalogue. This is particularly helpful to the client in understanding the planned qualities of the building. Rooms can be identified in groups or by the numbers required. For example, if all the floor coverings in the conference rooms in an office building are identical, floor coverings in other rooms can be unambiguously defined using this description

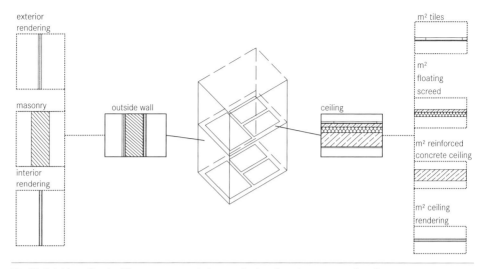

exterior rendering

masonry

interior rendering

outside wall

ceiling

m² tiles

m² floating screed

m² reinforced concrete ceiling

m² ceiling rendering

Fig. 25: Outside wall and ceiling as component elements broken down into construction elements

(e.g. "parquet floor, oak as in the conference rooms"). If the rooms are identified meticulously and fully, the building description will also work as a room schedule, as all the construction elements featuring in a room or group of rooms can be presented clearly. But a table in a construction element catalogue is considerably easier to work with than a room schedule.

Quantities for the construction element catalogue should be established as comprehensibly as possible in a table, so that synergies in deadline planning (duration of all processes) and, above all, quantity calculations can be exploited when going out to tender.

Establishing quantities for construction elements

If the appropriate cost figures are now added to the construction element catalogue, it is possible to proceed with determining the costs. The overall price for a construction element is then arrived at by multiplying the construction element quantity by the cost figure for the building element. The table can then simply be reorganised to calculate either costs for primary component elements or cost group, or also work categories.

Allocating cost figures

The chief advantage of costing based on construction element clearly lies in the additional use that can be made of the calculated costs by re-allocating them in budgets for tendering units for individual craft skills. The building description with construction elements makes it possible to define and adapt the qualities of the building as described more precisely even when the project is under way. Ultimately it forms the basis for draw-

Advantages and disadvantages of costing based on construction elements

Fig. 26: Construction elements catalogue (with cost groups allocated according to German standard DIN 276)

Cost group DIN 276	Construction element Description	Work type
350	**Ceilings**	
351	Reinforced concrete ceiling 20 cm, no requirements for under side of ceilings	Shell
352	Floating cement screed ZE20, thickness 50 mm on footfall insulation 20 mm, rest of structure in thermal insulation PS 20 WLG 035, total height 150 mm	Screed work
352	Parquet, wide oak plank, 22 mm, surface oiled in white	Parquet work
353	Gypsum rendering under the ceiling, average thickness 15 mm	Rendering work
340	**Interior walls**	
341	Reinforced concrete wall 15 cm, no surface requirements	Shell
345	Internal rendering on both sides, average thickness 15 mm	Rendering work

ing up the specifications for individual areas of work. Project-specific qualities, clearly summarised, are easier to understand for the client, as a layperson, than individual items in work specifications, as the construction element always describes the completed structural component and not the work necessary to manufacture it. Despite the high level of detail the structure remains very flexible, as each construction element can be allocated precisely to a cost group (e.g. in Germany according to the third level of DIN 276) and to a work area. > Chapter on terms and structures

COSTING BASED ON WORK SPECIFICATIONS

The degree of detail and precision within a cost calculation as described above can be increased considerably by breaking the component elements down into individual building elements. In order to makes things even more precise, it is possible to refine all the information about the individual construction elements that are relevant to cost within the specifications. A specification provides all the relevant information about the individual skills (trades) needed for realising the building, in the form of a set of textual building instructions. The construction element method focuses solely on the completed structure, but costs determined based on work specifications take the way in which the work is realised into account as well. In project-specific terms, the way in which the work is realised can influence costs considerably, as the wages element is correspondingly raised or lowered. These cost factors are not taken into account by the cost determination methods discussed so far.

All the construction elements in a building can be divided into individual service items, which can be summed up in corresponding specialist

Fig. 27: Construction element catalogue incl. allocation by room and quantity determination.

Cost group DIN 276	Construction element Description	Work type	Room groups Room numbers	Quantity Quantity unit
350	**Ceilings**			
351	Reinforced concrete ceiling 20 cm, no requirements for under side of ceilings	Shell	Offices and corridors	120 m²
352	Floating cement screed ZE20, thickness 50 mm on footfall sound insulation 20 mm. Rest of structure in thermal insulation PS 20 WLG 035, total height 150 mm.	Screed work	Offices and corridors	120 m²
352	Parquet, wide oak planking, 22 mm, surface oiled in white	Parquet work	Offices and corridors	120 m²
353	Gypsum rendering under the ceiling, average thickness 15 mm	Rendering work	Offices and corridors	120 m²
340	**Interior walls**			
341	reinforced concrete wall 15 cm, no surface requirements	Shell	Staircase	80 m²
345	Inner rendering on both sides, average thickness 15 mm	Rendering work	Staircase	160 m²

areas (trades). An example of this is shown in figure 29 for a tile and parquet floor and a loadbearing exterior wall.

○

A specification for laying parquet, for example, would list all the items necessary for preparing the completed floor, including ancillary items (all materials, protective measures, preparing the base, applying adhesive to the parquet, smoothing and oiling the parquet, fitting footboards etc.) for

Example: costing based on specifications

○ **Note:** When determining quantities for individual service items it is essential that the unit prices cited are all based on the same quantity calculation modalities. Different national approaches to calculation can be found here, and a variety of relevant rules can be found. In Germany, calculation modalities are laid down in VOB/C, for example. It may be necessary to convert the unit prices quoted for comparison. In the long term, sustainable documentation and evaluation of unit prices based on individual specification tenders makes it possible for the architect to achieve additional certainty when budgeting.

Fig. 28: Construction element catalogue incl. room allocation, quantity determination and cost figure allocation

Cost group	Construction element	Work type	Room groups	Quantity	Inclusive price	Total price
DIN 276	Description		Room numbers	Quantity unit	EUR/unit	EUR
350	**Decken**					**19,800.00**
351	Reinforced concrete ceiling 20 cm, no requirements for under side of ceilings	Shell	Offices and corridors	120 m²	87.00	10,440.00
352	Floating cement screed ZE20, thickness 50 mm on footfall sound insulation 20 mm. Rest of structure in thermal insulation PS 20 WLG 035, total height 150 mm.	Screed work	Offices and corridors	120 m²	16.00	1920.00
352	Parquet, wide oak planking, 22 mm, surface oiled in white	Parquet work	Offices and corridors	120 m²	47.00	5640.00
353	Gypsum rendering under the ceiling, average thickness 15 mm	Rendering work	Offices and corridors	120 m²	15.00	1800.00
340	**Interior walls**					**12,000.00**
341	Reinforced concrete wall 15 cm, no surface requirements	Shell	Staircase	80 m²	120.00	9600.00
345	Inner rendering on both sides, average thickness 15 mm	Rendering work	Staircase	160 m²	15.00	2400.00

the entire project on all floors. When the specification is complete, the architect can insert average unit prices for the individual items; multiplying them by the quantities determined will then give the total sum required for the parquet work. Once all the specifications for the different work needed to complete the building have been drawn up, the unit prices for the individual services can be added in as well. The individual specification totals then represent one tendering unit at the planning stage before the project is realised. Adding together all the specification totals with their unit prices gives a very realistic view of the total costs to be expected

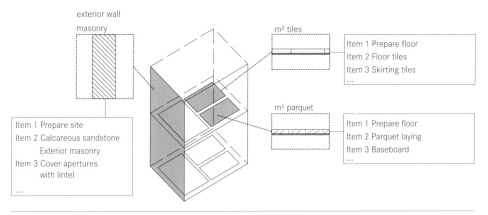

exterior wall

masonry

m² tiles

Item 1 Prepare floor
Item 2 Floor tiles
Item 3 Skirting tiles
...

Item 1 Prepare site
Item 2 Calcareous sandstone
    Exterior masonry
Item 3 Cover apertures
    with lintel
...

m² parquet

Item 1 Prepare floor
Item 2 Parquet laying
Item 3 Baseboard
...

Fig. 29: Construction elements broken down into individual service items

for the project as a whole. The specifications can then also be drawn up in a simplified form, with all the items defined by short titles only.

Costing based on specifications guarantees a reliably realistic statement about the costs to be expected. But this approach assumes that all the qualities and detailed requirements for the planning process have been finally fixed and that all the quantities have been listed without omissions. This means that the method cannot be used or does not provide reliable results in the absence of precise information about the realisation of the project. If planning for the project has not progressed far enough, another costing method should be used instead.

Account must also be taken of the fact that drawing up all the necessary specifications takes a comparatively long time, so the architect has to look at each project phase and decide whether the construction element or component element method might not be the right tool for determining the costs in this case. But if the planning is at a very advanced stage, no additional time will really be needed. On the contrary, costing based on specifications in fact anticipates planning work that the architect has to do anyway as part of putting building work out to tender. The work can be cut down to some extent by using simplified specifications, but the individual work items have to be expanded and adapted subsequently so that they can be used as a basis for seeking tenders from contractors.

Advantages and disadvantages of costing based on specifications

In particular cases, costing based on specifications can also be used in combination with other cost determination methods. Individual areas

Fig. 30: Costing for parquet work using a specification

Item no.	Work item Description	Quantity Unit	Unit price EUR	Total EUR
1	Clean the subsurface, remove of sinter layers	500 m²	5,00	2500
2	Glue oak planks 14 cm wide, 22 mm thick, light oak	500 m²	85.00	42,500
3	Oil parquet surface with white-pigmented oil	500 m²	10.00	5000
4	Fit footboard, 20 × 50 mm, MDF, white	500 m²	5.00	2500
5	Fixing skirting boards, 20 × 50 mm, MDF, white	100 m	12.00	1200
6	Cover completed parquet with protective cardboard	500 m²	2.50	1250
7	Apply tolerance compensation filler to concrete steps (110 × 30 cm)	50 Stk.	25.00	1250
8	Glue risers and steps, light oak, 3 cm × 110 cm × 30 cm or 17.5 cm, to match parquet	50 Stk.	150.00	7500
9	Smooth steps	50 Stk.	10.00	500
10	Oil steps with white-pigmented oil	50 Stk.	5.00	250
Parquet work total				**64,450**

of work for which wide-ranging information and thus certainty about planning are available can be described and priced sufficiently precisely based on specifications, whereas cost determination based on construction methods can make sense in other areas.

○ **Note:** If the architect is unable to find prices for rare or unusual construction elements in the literature, cost determination based on specifications still offers a possibility for putting one's own figure on a cost. In this way the individual items necessary for creating the construction element are determined and an inclusive price is reached using all the unit prices.

Continuing the budgeting process

There are no circumstances in which a building cost calculation that is set too low from the outset can produce a satisfactory outcome, as it will not be possible either to deliver the desired quality or to complete the full number of rooms required. This is why it is essential to conduct cost planning continuously and in stages in order to work within the project budget and thus keep the client satisfied. The foundation stone for this is laid when the project budget is first fixed. The following describes the project phases into which cost planning can be divided meaningfully and how the insights or results provided should be updated in the next project phase.

BASIC PRINCIPLES FOR CONTINUING AND MAINTAINING THE COST PLANNING PROCESS

As already described in the basic principles for cost planning chapter, the specified cost of keeping to the project budget is usually a key factor in the success of the project. Generally speaking, few points of detail have been settled at the time the decision to go ahead with the project is taken, so costings have to be updated throughout the planning and building process. Almost all the decisions made as the process continues – whether in terms of agreement about design, details, qualities or retrospective changes – will alter the cost structure of the process.

Costs must be fully presented at the point of each key decision by the commissioning client as the project proceeds and handed over as a basis for decisions along with the actual project documents such as plans, for example. The usual decision levels are:

Costing stages

1. Cost framework: deciding to go ahead with the project

The first step the architect takes is to establish whether the general conditions laid down by the client (site use, usable area, cost framework, timeline etc.) can be implemented in terms of the given requirements. In order to establish this s/he uses the development plans to examine whether the plot is suitable for such building and possible exploitation, and checks whether the costings and timeframe provided are realistic – without going as far as to produce a design. If it really is possible to realise a building within these project parameters, the necessary aids to decision-making are submitted to the client, who decides how the designs should be drawn up. This has major financial consequences, because the given parameters will form a basis for consulting and commissioning various building and specialist planners, and also experts in particular fields.

It is essential to check at this stage whether the specified cost and the desired usable area are statistically realistic, by reference to sample projects for which budgets have been calculated.

2. Estimating costs: deciding about the design idea/the preliminary design

After the architect has developed a first design idea s/he will present this to the client and, where appropriate, provide alternatives to help in making the decision. The client now has to decide whether to go ahead with the preliminary design, or which alternative should be pursued. In order to do this, s/he needs information about whether the design that has been devised can be realised within the specified cost, or which alternative will generate which construction costs. Fixing the design idea will make a considerable financial impact to the extent that approving the design represents a move towards design planning that might be acceptable for realisation, but basically is not being questioned in full.

So at this stage architects draw up the costs in with reference to the design by using volume- or area-related costings, or better by using costings that have already been compiled with reference to construction components/elements backed up by quantity surveying.

3. Calculating costs: deciding about submitting the application to build

Once the design has moved forward and been thoroughly planned to the extent that it is "adoption-ready", the client has to decide whether s/he wishes to realise it as presented, and so is ready submit the building application to the responsible authorities. In this respect, the building application generates facts, as the building permission granted on the basis of it reflects the design as it is to be realised, so if changes are required they have to be submitted to the authorities for approval.

At this stage, costs are compiled with reference to the design using cost figures based on construction components/elements backed by quantity surveying. This compilation is more detailed than at the last stage, as considerably more information about the project and the shape it is taking is available as a basis for costing.

4. Estimating costs: deciding to go to tender and fix the agreed construction work

After building permission is granted, preparations are made to put the building work out to tender, and for the actual realisation of the building. This is done drawing up descriptions of the work needed and where necessary providing final plans/details according to the chosen tendering and awarding procedure. Planning precision is enhanced by the degree of detail provided by the quality requirements in the tender's global description sections, and then by drawing on the detailed specifications, and this can lead to marked changes in the costs. After the documents have been submitted there is very little scope for making relevant changes, particularly in the case of public commissions. Thus fixing the "agreed construction work" is crucial within the tender process.

At this stage the costs are presented in terms of construction elements. This is based on structural components at first, by analogy with the level of detail in the tender documents, and is then reformulated with a view to contract award. So when single assignment awards are being made, budgets presented using single award units are easy to break down and easy to check when offers are submitted.

5. Comparing prices: deciding how to award the building work contract

After all the responses to the tender have come in and are available for consideration, the client has to decide which contractor s/he is going to commission to carry out the building work. The architect's examination of the tenders provides a basis for this: the client compares the prices and assesses deviations, variant solutions etc., and then makes a recommendation awarding the contract. Awarding the contract to a single contractor or to several single craft firms (trades) represents a significant milestone in the cost development, because after the contract has been awarded, any changes to the building programme have to be accounted for financially in consultation with the building firm. If the client takes out or cancels single items of work, payment still usually has to be made to the contractor, as the latter must receive either complete payment minus any saved expenditure or at least a profit claim based on the sum contracted.

The architect usually processes the tenders by comparing the single tender prices offered by the various contractors against each other. > Fig. 31

6. Establishing costs: determining the actual costs

Once all the building work is finished and audited and final accounts have been presented, the lead architect brings all the costs generated together in a cost statement. This is useful for the architect's own work on concluding the project, and also as information for the financing individuals or institutions or the client's auditors. So for example the bank providing the finance or an internal auditor on the client's side can check whether the monies that have been transferred have been used for the correct purposes in the building programme.

Fig. 31: Example of a price comparison

			Tender 1		Tender 2		
Item	Work involved	Quantity	Unit price	Total price	Unit price	Total price	...
01.001	Site preparation	Flat rate	EUR 200.00	EUR 200.00	EUR 450.00	EUR 450.00	
01.002	Ceiling rendering	60 m²	EUR 19.00	EUR 1140.00	EUR 22.00	EUR 1320.00	
01.003	Interior wall rendering	40 m²	EUR 25.00	EUR 1000.00	EUR 20.00	EUR 800.00	
01.003	Exterior wall rendering	40 m²	EUR 42.00	EUR 1680.00	EUR 46.00	EUR 1840.00	
01.004	...	...	...	...	...	...	...
...	...	...	...	...	...	...	...
...	...	...	...	...	...	...	...
	Total price						...

Fig. 32: Example of a list of decisions and changes

No.	Date	Decision/change	Approved/ rejected	Affects costs	Costs increased (+) Costs reduced (−)
1	10.03.14	Patterning on the tile product by client	yes	yes	EUR −1535.00
2	20.03.14	Change of tile colour	yes	no	0.00 EUR
3	25.04.14	Amendment 01 for compensating for the uneven ground	no	yes	EUR +2670.00
...	...	...	...	...	...

Cost control   Every cost determination stage is bound to deviate from its predecessor because new information has come to light, changes have been made or matters have become more concrete. So it is necessary to reconcile the current cost determination stage with the one before it and with the costs as originally specified. Here detailed reasons have to be supplied for any changes to the overall costs and how they can be picked up again if necessary. One way of presenting this via the planning and construction process is to produce a decision list and a list of changes, in which the main events after commissioning relevant to costs are listed chronologically. > Fig. 32

Sometimes the client or the project managers will insist that every decision or request for change by the client that is relevant to costs must be assessed and shown to the client. This makes for precise documentation of the cost-relevant processes.

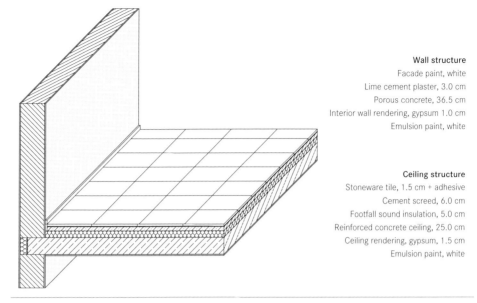

Wall structure
Facade paint, white
Lime cement plaster, 3.0 cm
Porous concrete, 36.5 cm
Interior wall rendering, gypsum 1.0 cm
Emulsion paint, white

Ceiling structure
Stoneware tile, 1.5 cm + adhesive
Cement screed, 6.0 cm
Footfall sound insulation, 5.0 cm
Reinforced concrete ceiling, 25.0 cm
Ceiling rendering, gypsum, 1.5 cm
Emulsion paint, white

Fig. 33: Structural detail for wall/ceiling

The aim is to put the client in a position to think over his or her deci- Controlling interventions
sions, and where appropriate to compensate for them by taking other measures. For example, this could entail reducing the quality of finish elsewhere, reducing the usable area or providing additional financial resources. It is essential here that the client be informed immediately or at a time close to the decision about which past arrangements have led to which consequences, and not simply be given a summary in a later project revision. So this work is not restricted to particular cost determi- nation stages, but must accompany the process and be carried out continuously.

WORKING WITH COST DETERMINATION BASED ON CONSTRUCTION ELEMENTS IN THE PLANNING PHASE

If a costing relating to construction elements is drawn up during the Groundwork in the preliminary design
design process, it will not usually contain much specific information about precise qualities and surface finishes. This is because materials and sur- face qualities tend to be decided on successively in the course of the planning process. So in the first place costs are worked out by working on general assumptions about quality. > Figs. 33 and 34

Component		Quantity	Unit	Inclusive price (EUR/unit)	Total price
Ceiling					
	Tiles	60	m²	80	EUR 4800.00
	Floating screed	60	m²	25	EUR 1500.00
	Reinforced concrete ceiling	60	m²	115	EUR 6900.00
	Rendering	60	m²	19	EUR 1140.00
	Paint	60	m²	4	EUR 240.00
				Total	**EUR 14,580.00**
Wall					
	Facade paint	40	m²	13	EUR 520.00
	Exterior rendering	40	m²	42	EUR 1680.00
	Masonry	40	m²	105	EUR 4200.00
	Interior rendering	40	m²	25	EUR 1000.00
	Interior paintwork	40	m²	4	EUR 160.00
				Total	**EUR 7560.00**

Clients will often have said nothing at all about individual materials or quality, so that the architect has to set a first general quality standard. The client will then see from these listings what standard the architect is working from, and what general quality standards the architect has used when determining the construction costs.

Continuing the planning process

Decisions are made and details are regularly clarified throughout the planning process, in meetings with the client, for example, so that these can then be incorporated into the current costing. > Fig. 35 Cost changes can then be identified directly and passed on to the client by matching

● the qualities laid down in the list to the relevant costing figures.

● **Example:** In the exploratory phase of the preliminary design, decisions made by the client and the architect are usually based on broad creative themes within the design. But then the client says that she or he wants to see a "good average standard". Then the architect, when determining costs, will accept simple parquet as a floor covering, without any further specific details at first, tiles costing an average sum, and gypsum rendering, painted white, for the surface finish.

Fig. 35: Concrete detail for cost determination based on construction elements

Component	Construction element	Quantity	Unit	Inclusive price (EUR/unit)	Total price
Ceiling					
	Stoneware tile 30 × 60 cm, anthracite, laid using the thin bed method, grouting in tile shade, skirting tiles	60	m²	80	EUR 4800.00
	Cement screed as floating hot screed, d = 6 cm, on 5 cm footfall sound insulation	60	m²	25	EUR 1500.00
	Reinforced concrete ceiling, in-situ concrete, d = 25 cm, shuttering, reinforcement, underbeams	60	m²	115	EUR 6900.00
	Sprayed ceiling rendering, gypsum rendering, d = 1.5 cm, pre-treatment of floor	60	m²	19	EUR 1140.00
	Indoor emulsion paint, ceiling, white	60	m²	4	EUR 240.00
				Total	**EUR 14,580.00**
Wall					
	Exterior paint for mineral substrates, white	40	m²	13	EUR 520.00
	Exterior wall rendering, lime cement plaster, d = 3.0 cm, pre-treatment of floor	40	m²	42	EUR 1680.00
	Masonry wall, porous concrete, d = 36.5 cm	40	m²	105	EUR 4200.00
	Interior wall rendering, gypsum plaster, d = 1.5 cm, pre-treatment of floor	40	m²	25	EUR 1000.00
	Interior emulsion paint, wall, light colour	40	m²	4	EUR 160.00
				Total	**EUR 7560.00**

With this approach the continuation of the costing becomes an iterative planning component because planning decisions are constantly checked, adapted and modified by feedback from the cost management process until a viable solution is found that does justice to the budget. Continuation to the end of the planning phase produces a final project target as a basis for going out to and awarding tender.

Fig. 36: Costing based on contract award

Trade	Construction element	Quantity	Inclusive price (EUR/unit)	Total price
Shell				EUR 11,100.00
	Reinforced concrete ceiling, in-situ concrete, d = 25 cm, shuttering, reinforcement, underbeams	60 m²	115.00	EUR 6900.00
	Masonry wall, porous concrete, d = 36.5 cm	40 m²	105.00	EUR 4200.00
Rendering work				EUR 3820.00
	Sprayed ceiling rendering, gypsum rendering, d = 1.5 cm, pre-treatment of floor	60 m²	19.00	EUR 1140.00
	Sprayed ceiling rendering, gypsum rendering, d = 1.5 cm, pre-treatment of floor	40 m²	25.00	EUR 1000.00
	Exterior wall rendering, lime cement plaster, d = 3.0 cm, pre-treatment of floor	40 m²	42.00	EUR 1680.00
Painting				EUR 920.00
	Interior emulsion paint, wall, light colour	40 m²	4.00	EUR 160.00
	Indoor emulsion paint, ceiling, white	60 m²	4.00	EUR 240.00
	Exterior paint for mineral substrates, white	40 m²	13.00	EUR 520.00
Screed work				EUR 1500.00
	Cement screed as floating hot screed, d = 6 cm, on 5 cm footfall sound insulation	60 m²	25.00	EUR 1500.00
Tiling				EUR 4800.00
	Stoneware tile 30 × 60 cm, anthracite, laid using the thin bed method, grouting in tile shade, skirting tiles	60 m²	80.00	EUR 4800.00
			Total	EUR 22,140.00

WORKING WITH TRADE-ORIENTED COST DETERMINATION IN THE TENDERING PHASE

Tender-oriented view

The continuing process of establishing costs changes once the tender documents are drawn up. Up to this point the design and the construction components associated with it have essentially provided the focus, but now definite building jobs are being assigned to one or more contractors, and they will determine the relevant structuring for the costing process.

Fig. 37: Matching up budgets and contract award sums

Trade	Construction element	Quantity	Inclusive price (EUR/unit)	Total price/budget	Contract award price	Deviation
Shell				**EUR 11,100.00**	**EUR 11,460.00**	**EUR +360.00**
	Reinforced concrete ceiling, in-situ concrete, d = 25 cm, shuttering, reinforcement, underbeams	60 m²	115.00	EUR 6900.00	EUR 7140.00	EUR +240.00
	Masonry wall, porous concrete, d = 36.5 cm	40 m²	105.00	EUR 4200.00	EUR 4320.00	EUR +120.00
Rendering work				**EUR 3820.00**	**EUR 3620.00**	**EUR −200.00**
	Sprayed ceiling rendering, gypsum rendering, d = 1.5 cm, pre-treatment of floor	60 m²	19.00	EUR 1140.00	EUR 1020.00	EUR −120.00
	Sprayed ceiling rendering, gypsum rendering, d = 1.5 cm, pre-treatment of floor	40 m²	25.00	EUR 1000.00	EUR 1080.00	EUR +80.00
	Exterior wall rendering, lime cement plaster, d = 3.0 cm, pre-treatment of floor	40 m²	42.00	EUR 1680.00	EUR 1520.00	EUR −160.00
...	...	...	...	...	...	...

So the costing table, which has previously been based on structural components, is re-sorted so that the individual structural components are subordinated to the contract units or trades. As described in the chapter on costing methods, costing based on construction elements, the essential requirement is that each construction element can be properly allocated as a structural component, or to a trade as a contract award unit.

Summing up the individual structural elements as a contract award unit makes it possible to create contract award budgets that can be compared directly when submitting and assessing the offers. This listing forms the basis for keeping an eye on costs throughout the building phase.

Creating contract award budgets

If a contract is awarded to individual craftspeople, then over- or under-spending on the contract award budget as calculated can be compensated for by subsequent contract awards during the building process. > Fig. 38

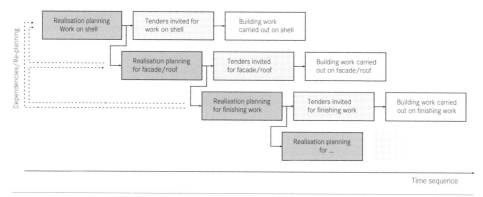

Fig. 38: Typical sequence for planning and contract award during the building phase

COST CONTROL IN THE BUILDING PHASE

When the building contract is awarded the building costs are fixed via the contractual payment agreement as a lump sum, or a provisional one (in the case of settlement or unit price contracts).

○ This makes it necessary to update and check costs throughout the building period. The client must be informed of significant cost changes immediately so that she or he can intervene to direct matters where appropriate. But minor cost changes are normal, and do not necessarily need intervention and direction.

Structuring cost control

The following cost control sequence is triggered by each award unit:
1. Fixing the budget
2. Invitation to tender and submission of offers
3. Assessment and checking of the contract award sum with the budget specification
4. Cost predictions and cost control during the building process
5. Following up changes in the scope or content of work
6. Cost statement after checking the final invoice

> Chapter on working with trade-referenced cost determination in the contract award phase

Sequence of events with single tenders

If contracts for the building work are awarded to several firms, this scheme makes it possible to check on each individual contractor in terms of costs. This is because the contractors are all appointed at different times. So it can come about in the course of the building process that individual items of work (e.g. earthworks, shell construction) have been paid off, but later items have not yet even gone out to tender and been awarded. Other jobs may still be in progress. If a current cost estimate

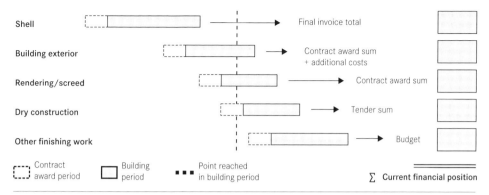

Fig. 39: Working out the current financial position during the building phase

is to be made now, then very different situations in terms of contracts awarded and work completed will have to be taken into account. If work has been completed, the final invoice sum will be used here, but where work is still in hand the contract award sums plus known additional costs and deviations from the original agreement in terms of work done will form the basis. Work that has still not gone out to tender will continue within the budget as calculated. As soon as offers or a commission are available, the appropriate sums will be taken from the contract. > Fig. 39

This produces a work-related table of costs that can be continued on the basis of the contract-award related costing. The most up-to-date cost data for a piece of work are listed in the last column, so that the sum of this column reflects the current financial position. > Fig. 40

Checking contractors' invoices can reveal that the bills of quantities as originally accepted clearly differ from the quantities invoiced. Any quantity deviations for items affecting costs should feature in the table of costs.

Information gained from checking the invoice

○ **Note:** In the case of a unit price contract, payment is made according to the amount of work done. Consolidating payment into a lump sum shifts the risk in relation to quantities to the contractor. This depends on the degree of detail provided in the description of the agreed construction work.

● **Example:** Quite often the ground to be built on is checked only by random test drillings prior to the work. The resultant assumptions about quantities can turn out to be wrong once soil starts to be excavated. If this occurs, the costs should be adjusted correspondingly in the case of unit price contracts.

Fig. 40: Structure of a costs table during the building phase

Job/ contract award unit	Structural elements	Quantity/ units	Budget cost estimate	Contract award sum	Additional costs/Cost prediction	Final invoice	Current financial position
Job 1	Construction element 1						
	Construction element 2						

Incorporating additional sums

It is not unusual for work to be listed that is not included in the "agreed construction work", perhaps because it was forgotten when the work went out to tender, was not open to identification, came to light only in the building phase, or was ordered by the client at a later stage. Sums that deviate from the "agreed construction work" (also know as additional payments), can be generated as modifications to work required or delays during the building period, as well as by the above-mentioned quantity deviations. Changes to work required include all changes ordered by the client, plus necessary work, exclusions/partial terminations etc. Costs generated by delays during the building period mean all the additional costs resulting from obstacles to the building process, extending or speeding up the building period.

Demands from contractors for additional payments are checked against the grounds for the claim, whether it is justified, and the amount involved. As a rule, the additional price must correspond with the contract price level. This means that if a contractor has stated a very reasonable price in the tender, the additional price must be correspondingly low. Additional charges are then included in the table of costs, and here it is also possible to distinguish between checked, unchecked and assigned charges. For large projects, separate lists of additional charges are usually kept, and these record and evaluate all additional charges so far incurred chronologically. The totals for all these lists of additional charges are then transferred into the statement of costs.

Cost predictions

But it is not only additional costs that make the building process more expensive. Often the site manager will notice things that have not yet been addressed but will or could generate additional costs as the building process moves on. For example, if items were omitted from the invitation to tender, then the costs generated should be built into the cost predictions as soon as they are identified – even if the contractor concerned has not yet made an additional charge.

Fig. 41: Established costs for the client based on contracts as awarded

Job/contract award unit	Total final invoice
Work on shell	EUR 512,134.50
Roof waterproofing work	EUR 64,478.42
Windows	EUR 83,210.00
Rendering	EUR 51,619.36
Rendering work	EUR 12,820.00
Dry construction	EUR 21,143.67
Painting	EUR 10,405.50
Heating/plumbing	EUR 134,685.08
...	...
Total construction costs	**EUR 1,105,680.05**

ESTABLISHING AND ASSESSING COSTS

Once the project has been inspected, approved, and any necessary corrective measures taken, the contractors involved in the project will present their final invoices within a contractually agreed period. These will include all the costs generated by the project on the basis of contractually agreed additional payments, and those that have emerged subsequently. The final invoices are checked for correctness by the architect and amended where applicable.

The costing that documents the actual project costs (> Chapter on the basic approach to updating and serving cost planning) is made up of the sum of all the costs incurred and thus represents a survey of all the costs already generated, and represents the final cost determination stage. Usually a list of all the costs in the final invoices is drawn up here and presented as a total sum, and this is usually sufficient information in terms of the client's interest.

Total of all final invoices

If the table structure for the planning and construction process had been updated systematically, the contract-based totals can be re-allocated to the original construction elements without a great deal of effort. This has distinct advantages for the architect, as it means that he or she can assess the project as a whole and thus draw conclusions and determine costs for future projects.

Re-organisation based on structural components

To do this, the sums actually invoiced, including all changes, additional charges etc. are divided by quantities invoiced. When compiling cost figures based on construction elements, care must be taken that all

Compiling cost figures

Fig. 42: Determining costing figures

Job/contract award unit	Heading	Sum due under heading	Quantity invoiced	Inclusive price cost figure
Dry construction				
	Dry-built walls	EUR 24,154.50	517.56 m²	approx. EUR 47.00/m²
	Firewalls	EUR 3468.36	46.50 m²	approx. EUR 75.00/m²
	Suspended ceilings	EUR 11,210.42	214.67 m²	approx. EUR 52.00/m²
	...	...		

the additional constituent elements are added in again. This can be done most successfully if all the essential building components including relevant secondary items are listed under their own headings in the invitations to tender. In this way the specific value can be derived from the invoiced sum under this heading and the total quantity under the main item. > Fig. 42

If specific values are to be prepared for component elements, the relevant costs should be totalled from a retrospective cost breakdown based on building parts. To compile costings relating to volume or area, the invoiced construction costs should be divided by the areas and gross cubic capacity that will usually have been determined previously for the building application.

○ **Note:** It is important for planning practices to set up their own costing databases. Costs derived from their own projects define costs according to the individual quality requirements, constructions and degrees of detail customary for the practice, and are therefore significantly more precise than average statistical values that are generally accessible.

■ **Tip:** Costings should always be entered in a personal database without value added tax, in case this is altered by law. It also makes sense to name the construction year as well, so that cost values can still be used by allowing for inflation and statistical adjustments. Statistics offices in almost all countries keep records of significant price fluctuations in the building sector.

In conclusion

Construction costs are a key element for the client in almost all architectural projects, and determine their success or failure. The aesthetic quality of a building is very important, but it is governed by subjective evaluation criteria – as a layperson, the client can judge a building technically only to a limited extent. But apart from the user-friendliness of a building, keeping to costs and where necessary to deadlines are fixed factors that are extremely important for the client, who can also assess them very readily. Keeping within the planned building costs can always be checked in terms of concrete figures. High creative ambitions and good architectural concepts can be realised and implemented attractively only if they are based on professional budgeting. This ensures that the desired quality will be delivered, but also guarantees that the project as whole is financially viable, and no architecture can be realised if this does not happen. So it is essential for architects to see the subject of costs as an essential planning element, to tie the emerging designs and projects together in a structured way, and to cost them carefully.

Even though the subject of costs is often not an important feature of architectural studies, a competent approach to costs is essential if architects are to be successful in their later professional lives. For this reason the methods and practical procedures are an important building block in architectural studies as a preparation for their subsequent professional lives. Understanding creative design, technical construction, holistic co-ordination and competent budgeting as an iterative process constitutes a good architect's repertoire. Just as the design process cannot be schematised, budgeting is also a project-related heterogeneous process that adapts itself both to the client's special needs and spheres of interest and also understands how to illustrate the shape of a particular project and its specific idiosyncrasies.

Appendix

LITERATURE

Bert Bielefeld, Lars-Philip Rusch: *Building projects in China,* Birkhäuser Verlag, Basel 2006

Bert Bielefeld, Falk Würfele: *Building projects in the European Union,* Birkhäuser Verlag, Basel 2005

Chartered Institute of Building (ed.): *Planning and Programming in Construction,* Chartered Institute of Building, London 1991

CIRIA: *The Environmental Handbooks for Building and Civil Engineering: Vol 1. Design and Specification,* Thomas Telford Ltd, 1994

Sandra Christensen Weber: *Scheduling Construction Projects. Principles and Practices,* Pearson Prentice Hall, Upper Saddle River, NJ, 2005

Institution of Civil Engineers, Association of Consulting Engineers and Civil Engineering Contractors Association: *Tendering for Civil Engineering Contracts,* Thomas Telford Ltd, 2000

Richard H. Neale, David E. Neale: *Construction Planning,* Telford, London 1989

Jay S. Newitt: *Construction Scheduling. Principles and Practices,* Pearson Prentice Hall, Upper Saddle River, NJ, 2009

THE AUTHORS

Bert Bielefeld, Prof. Dr.-Ing. Architect, architect teaches construction economics and construction management at Siegen University and is managing partner of the bertbielefeld&partner architecture practice in Dortmund.

Roland Schneider, Dipl.-Ing. M.Sc. Architect, is academic assistant in the construction economics and construction management department at Siegen University and managing director of the art-schneider architecture practice in Cologne.

Thanks go to Ann Christin Hecker and Benjamin Voss for their support in creating the graphics.

Series editor: Bert Bielefeld
Conception: Bert Bielefeld, Annette Gref
Translation from German into English:
Michael Robinson
English copy editing: Monica Buckland
Layout and cover design: Andreas Hidber
Typesetting and production: Amelie Solbrig
Project management: Annette Gref

A CIP catalogue record for this book is available
from the Library of Congress, Washington D.C.,
USA.

Bibliographic information published by the
German National Library
The German National Library lists this publica-
tion in the Deutsche Nationalbibliografie;
detailed bibliographic data are available on the
Internet at http://dnb.dnb.de.

This book is also available in a German language
edition (ISBN 978-3-03821-530-1).

© 2014 Birkhäuser Verlag GmbH, Basel
P.O. Box 44, 4009 Basel, Switzerland
Part of De Gruyter

Printed on acid-free paper produced from
chlorine-free pulp. TCF ∞

Printed in Germany

ISBN 978-3-03821-532-5

9 8 7 6 5 4 3 2 1

www.birkhauser.com